The Antics of a PK (Preacher's Kid) And The Devotions To Try To Justify Them

Debby Hadley Triplett

Published by Debby Hadley Triplett, 2024.

While every precaution has been taken in the preparation of this book, the publisher assumes no responsibility for errors or omissions, or for damages resulting from the use of the information contained herein.

THE ANTICS OF A PK (PREACHER'S KID) AND THE DEVOTIONS TO TRY TO JUSTIFY THEM

First edition. November 21, 2024.

Copyright © 2024 Debby Hadley Triplett.

ISBN: 979-8230956884

Written by Debby Hadley Triplett.

I would like to dedicate this book to my parents. They are both in Heaven now but, after writing this book I'm sure they lost a lot of sleep because of me.

First grade must have been a banner year for me.

LET'S SET THE STAGE:

We're going back eight years before I was born. This I'm sure, was a trying time for my parents. This was before my dad was a minister.

I had a sister named Barbara Kay. She was the first born. She was a true doll baby, for sure.

My dad was going to a men's prayer group. Every time he prayed that his father would come to know God as his true savior.

One night he prayed, "whatever it takes." When he got home, he told my mom what he had prayed. She just looked at him and asked him if he really was willing to take what might happen with that kind of prayer.

A few months later, Barbara became sick and was hospitalized. The diagnosis was an enlarged heart. It wasn't long until she died.

On the day of her funeral, my grandfather walked in the door and hung his Stetson on a hook. He paused and speaking to no one in the room he said "I guess it's time for me to get right with the Lord". He was led in the sinner's prayer and became very active in the church. He served very faithfully for many years.

DEVOTION

Through him you believe in God, who raised him from the dead and glorified him, and so your faith and hope are in God. 1 Peter 1:21 NIV

Knowing what my parents went through, I have never said, whatever it takes. I have never lost a child and I never presume to know how my parents felt.

I have lost two husbands and know the sting of death. At this point in your life, you don't know what is going on around you. Life goes on and you look at people and ask, don't you understand the happened.

What about life after a spouse dies? Things change, you are no longer a couple. You feel like a third wheel around couples with whom you ran around.

If you choose to, after grieving, you get to remake yourself into a new person. You are able to achieve things you thought you could only dream. It might take years, if you let it happen, happiness sneaks back into your life and you realize you can go on. It takes trusting God to use this to his good. It's not easy but, you can go on.

Father, I may not know the loss of a child but, death has come into my life. I chose to move on but, there are those who can't. Help them to see there is life to be lived and love that can still be shared. AMEN

LET'S SET THE STAGE:

Now a story I get to tell on my brother! I bet they thought I would make this all about me. I can't in all fairness leave them out.

Oh, my brother used to make me so mad. Yes, it shocks me that I admitted that too! He was as big a stinker as I. Well, almost, he did learn a few things not to do from me.

He told lies left and right. On the times he got caught, he would just add "can't you take a joke". How can a parent respond to that? In the end, he never got in trouble. He would say, "I was just joking."

One time my mom had just about had it with "Can't you take a joke?" Before she could stop herself, she said "I hope when you have kids of your own, they say that to you."

Fast forward into adulthood and life as a father. David and his son were at my mom's and dad's house. David caught Nick in a little lie. Nick didn't know about when David was young. He was getting on to him and Nick said "Can't you take a joke?" My mom had to excuse herself to her bedroom to laugh. That my people is justice pure and simple. David got his come uppance!

I'm not sure about any "whoopin's" then.

DEVOTION

**Truthful lips endure forever, but a lying tongue is but for a moment.
Proverbs 12:19**

If I were being truthful here, since it was my brother, there were so many verses I wanted to use. I'll, try to be a little nicer now.

In all ways we should tell the truth. I know in our society little white lies are ok. But, are they? It doesn't matter how big or small a lie; a lie is a lie in God's eyes.

Let's look at those little white lies. You may think It was of no consequence whether you did or didn't do what they asked you. You might feel you need these people to see you in a little better light. That you need make you look good. Maybe you just can't admit you did that little thing. Is any of this sounding familiar? That little lie you told is as bad as the big one you would never tell.

Father, help us always be mindful of our mouth. What we say or do have such an impact on others. While it might not be that big of a deal to us, in your eyes we have sinned as bad as murderer. Amen

LET'S SET THE STAGE:

When this happened, I was in first grade. Back then I was very accident prone. That has never stopped being true into my adulthood.

Bear in mind, that at the time of this writing, I am well into my retirement. The games we played when I was in first grade is a far cry from today's playground games.

We were playing Red Rover. We all lined up into 2 teams lined up facing each other. We held hands in line and yelled Red Rover, Red Rover send Debby right over. I would take off and try to break the line. This one day I was chasing a boy (don't ask me, I was six) he fell and I fell on top of him and I broke my arm. I know! How in the world was I the one with the broken arm? Well, as we fell, I got my arm underneath him and I was the one that got hurt. This won't be the last story of my broken bones.

This ended up with me going to the doctor and getting a cast on my arm. I really thought it was cool because everyone got to sign my cast. I really enjoyed being the center of attention.

DEVOTION

A third time the LORD called, 'Samuel!' And Samuel got up and went to Eli and said, 'Here I am; you called me.' Then Eli realized that the LORD was calling the boy. 1 Sameul 3:8

Most of us are familiar with the story of Sameul hearing God calling him and thinking it was Eli. It wasn't until the third time that Eli realized it was God calling him.

Are we always being mindful of the voice of God? Are we so in tune in our daily lives that we can recognize the voice of God. In our daily walk with God, do we listen to that still small voice?

How do you use the gifts God has given you, how about that calling on your life? Do you even recognize when God is speaking to you in that still small voice. What is God telling you to do. My pastor used the illustration the other Sunday and pointed out someone in the congregation and said "God telling you to give that waitress a $100 tip." We want signs from God as confirmation. We need to stay in tune and in companionship with our Lord so we just do what he wants.

Father, help us to draw ever closer to you so we can recognize your voice. Help us to be mindful of you enough to just do what you have asked us to do. AMEN

LET'S SET THE STAGE:

I'm 5 and we still live in the country. My dad worked in St Louis and was only home on the weekend.

While my dad was in St Louis, I realized I wanted to be saved. I know some people believe children this age aren't old enough to understand what they are doing but, I have, since that day, understood the meaning of being saved.

My mom knew my dad would want to be the one to lead me in the sinner's prayer. I was already in bed when my dad got home but, he came in and I was saved that night in my bedroom.

On Saturday Daddy told me that I could come before the church to profess my faith on Sunday night. I don't remember why I had to wait until Sunday night, but I did.

Sunday night we went through the whole service. I couldn't wait until the end of the service so I could go forward.

Well, my dad forgot to hold an invitation that night and he dismissed everyone. As we were leaving the church, I asked my dad why I couldn't come forward that night. He stopped everyone heading to their cars and asked them to come back. Everyone came back, puzzled by what was happening. My dad told everyone that I had something to say. I told them that I got saved and I wanted to be baptized. I was baptized in the Gasconade River. By now those sins are gone to be seen never again.

DEVOTION

For God so loved the world that he gave his one and only Son, that whoever believes in him shall not perish but have eternal life. NIV

Where are you in your walk with God? Have you given you life and accepted the mercy and graciousness of our Lord Jesus Christ.

God sent his son as a tiny infant to this Earth to be sacrificed for us. John the Baptist baptized Jesus and the Holy Spirit descended as a dove as proof he was truly the Son of God. His ministry started when he was thirty at the age of thirty three, He was crucified for the atonement of our sins.

Within one week, he went from being heralded upon entering Jerusalem; to arrest and charged because He said He was the Son of God. At this time, He was turned over to the ruler Pilate. His wife warned him of a dream she had that Jesus was a righteous man. Pilate would make no decision about the fate of Jesus and gave into the bidding of the people who were yelling, "Crucify him, crucify him." He was turned over to be scourged. "A scourge is a short whip with knots tied in the ends with bones or metal tied to the end to tear the skin of the criminals". When they were done his muscles were exposed and he was almost dead. Then they made Jesus carry his cross to Calvary. Stumbling, they got Simon of Cyrene, a man that came to Jerusalem for Passover, to finish carrying His cross. He laid on the cross with nails in his hands and his feet. As the day progressed, they took a spear and put it into his side. When this had taken place Jesus said, "Father forgive them for they don't know what they are doing," and he died.

It did not end there; on the end of third day, He came up out of the sealed grave to prove He was truly the Son of God.

If you haven't done so, please say this prayer to accept Jesus to be the Lord of your life.

Father, please forgive me of my sins, come into my life that I might live with you throughout eternity. I understand that you sent your Son as a tiny infant and He willingly gave His life for the atonement of the sins we commit. Walk with me in this journey and help me to become the example you need me to be. Let my life shine with your love and graciousness. AMEN

LET'S SET THE STAGE:

I'm still infirst grade except we moved from the country into St Louis. I was kind of the teacher's pet in the country because my aunt was a first grade teacher and Mrs. Brown was good friends with her. After being the teacher's pet, I really thought my new teacher was MEAN. I really didn't like her.

One morning I got up and decided I wasn't going to school. My sister tried to warn me, BUT NOOO! I just wasn't going. I just didn't think it through. We lived on one end of the block and my grandparents on the other.

I'm not exactly sure how my mom found out I wasn't going to school. I was probably playing in the backyard. I was only in first grade after all. I was not at all worldly.

I remember my mom coming down and yelling at me. I took off, that was my second mistake. My brother was a toddler, and she went up and called my grandpa and he came outside to try to catch me. My mom also had to leave my brother alone in the apartment; another strike against me. They came after me from both ends of the street. Every time they thought they had me cornered, I would dart through someone's yard between the sidewalk and the alley. This went on for about 5 minutes or so.

Yep, as you can probably guessed they finally caught me. My grandpa went to the apartment and got my brother and took him home with him. My mom promptly took off taking me to that school building.

Let me just say, that was the longest walk of my life. Three or four city blocks. I can't really say I was walking exactly. You see, my feet were only hitting the ground about every two steps. My mom's hand was making contact with my butt and it lifted me off the ground. ALL THE WAY TO SCHOOL!

Remember how mean I said the teacher was? She was less than pleased to have to stop the lesson to get me from my mom. She came to the door with such a look and I'm sure she was going to give me "what for", that was until she saw the tears on my face and the look on my mom's face. Let me just say that even into high school I never skipped school again.

Disclaimer: This is the story from the memory of a six year-old. I never had the courage to ask my mom about that one.

DEVOTION

For since the message spoken through angels was binding, and every violation and disobedience received it's just punishment. Hebrews 2:2

I really thought this verse was fitting the story. How about our lives.

After accepting Christ as our savior, how do we live our own lives? As a follower of Christ, we are to live a life fitting of that title. Sin makes its way in where we should never let it. How we respond is the difference. Our attitude makes all the difference.

Well, that one little thing I did won't make that much of a difference. That one word we said, that one lie we told and for some, that one person we hurt or killed. All sins are equal in God's sight.

Let's all be ever mindful of the way we live our lives.

Father, none of us are perfect. Only you are perfect but, help us to strive to make a conscious effort to live a life befitting you and all that you did to give us eternal life. Let our lives be an example to the world that we are your chosen. AMEN

LET'S SET THE STAGE:

First grade must have been a banner year for me because again, I'm in first grade in this one. We lived in an upstairs apartment where the dining room, my parents' bedroom, the living room and the hall made one big circle.

One night after supper my dad saw that the tooth that was loose was just barely hanging on. He called me over and told me to open my mouth. I'm sure by now you can guess my response. I just clenched my jaw and closed my mouth and the fight ensued.

Somehow, I got loose from my dad and the chase was on! I'm not sure how many circles we made around that apartment. I do know the longer I ran the more trouble I was in! My dad was six foot and had a very loud walk. I'm not sure what the neighbor's downstairs thought was going on. I do remember going under my parent's bed and him going over the bed and round and round we went. I don't remember how I got caught but, I did.

After he got me, I was laid on the floor and he put his knees on both sides of me and again tried to get into my mouth. Again, he was met with that clinched jaw and pursed lips. I didn't win that battle because with just a little help the tooth fell out. I don't think it even bled.

OH YEAH, I GOT A WHOOPIN!

DEVOTION

But Jonah ran away from the LORD and headed for Tarshish. He went down to Joppa, where he found a ship bound for that port. After paying the fare, *he went aboard and sailed for Tarshish to flee* from the LORD. Jonah 1:3

Are you running from something? What plans does God have for you?

Have you got a calling on your life or a gift He has given to you that you aren't fulfilling

God has plans for all of us from the time we were conceived. He sees from the beginning to the end but, we indeed have free will. We sometimes get side tracked from his original plan.

What will it take for you to get back on the right path. Maybe you are just taking a break and it's time to get back on the path that was chosen for you.

Father, let us always do the things you have planned for us. Help us to see those things more clearly and give us the strength to step up to fulfill our destiny. AMEN

LET'S SET THE STAGE:

My life has progressed a little bit here. I was in second grade still in that same apartment. Here is how the bathroom was set up. You walk in and the tub is on the right and the commode was at the end and a pedestal sink about three feet from the commode. This is really important in this story.

It was Spring and getting warm outside. Of course, at the mere sign of Spring, I had to take my shoes off to play outside. Now, I still wear a sweatshirt.

I got called in to eat supper. We started to eat and I guess my mom got a glimpse of how dirty my feet were. She looked at me and said "Deborah Ann, get in that bathroom and wash those feet." She said my whole name so I knew she meant business.

Any normal person would have gone in that bathroom, put their feet in the tub and washed their feet. Not me! Of course, I never did things the normal way. Don't you wash your hands in the sink? That seems the way to go this time. I got on the commode and stretched all the way across to the sink. Don't you think that sounds reasonable? I got my feet clean as a whistle. It wasn't until it was time to get down. I stood up to retrace my steps and splat, I fell to the floor. You know I told you there would be more broken bones and sure enough off to the hospital we went. I broke my collarbone this time.

I probably got a hamburger and not a whoopin'!

DEVOTON

But everything exposed by the light becomes visible—and everything that is illuminated becomes a light. Ephesians 5:13

I'm just coming out of a very hard three years. My husband died, I moved to my hometown I swore I would never return to and then my apartment flooded and I lost over worth thirty thousand dollars' worth of stuff. Then I moved about three and a half hours north.

Are you wondering how I see things in a very bright light? It has taken me three years but things are starting to look up. I'm no longer in my hometown. I moved close to where I grew up and am comforted by the fact that I'm surrounded by friends I have known for fifty five years. I remade myself into the person God wants for this stage of my life. I am a part of a church that is not just a church but, a family that walks the talk of the brightness of the Lord. Hard times happen, and this won't be the last hard time. I know that God has me in the hard times as much as he has me good times. He makes these promises in His Word.

Father, help us understand that even in the hard times you are there. You only want the best for us and in the end, things that look like the are so out of control, circle back and you make all things good.

LET'S SET THE STAGE:

Mom and Dad bought a house. We moved into it when I was in second grade. I would say this story took place in the Spring of second grade. The month was May.

My Mom and Dad told us we were going to a St Louis Cardinal's game then off to my cousin Connie's house. I really liked going to the ballgame, (still do). So much for my mind to see and think about doing.

After the game was over, we went to my Grandparents house. Now, I loved them very much but, it was not Connie's house. I just kept going over to my mom and asking when we were going to Connie's. My mom was not cooperating at all in my mind. Finally, my mom said, "let's head to Doris". Now she's speaking my language! We all loaded up into cars.

My sister always loved to ride with our Aunt Marie, everyone else rode with Mom and Dad.

We pulled up to Connie's and when we got out of the car my mom and aunt asked at the same time "Where's Papa" What I didn't know was it was Grandpa's birthday and they were giving him a surprise party. At least a surprise until I kept asking when we were going to Connie's. My mom and my aunt both thought the other had my grandpa. We were at a surprise party without the birthday boy. Aunt Marie was headed to the car to go get him when he pulled up. Guess it was a good thing I kept pressing my mom to go to Connie's. We were about to have a birthday party without the guest of honor. OOPS!

No Whoopin'! For this one time, everyone was glad I was so insistent.

DEVOTION

**Look, I come like a thief! Blessed is the one who stays awake and remains clothed, so as not to go naked and be shamefully exposed.'
Revelation 16:15**

Ever since Jesus went back to Heaven, people have been saying the end of time is here. These days, signs are pointing more and more that way. It doesn't matter if you believe that Jesus' return is soon or not, every day that passes it is one more day closer.

The way we live our lives is vital. Matthew 25 is the parable of the ten virgins. five of the virgins have plenty of oil for their lamps and five run out of oil. The ones that ran out asked for oil from the others to keep their lamps lit.

This parable symbolized the second coming of Jesus. The five were ready and the others were not. Are you living your life prepared for Jesus' return? We should walk daily with Christ like today is the last day we are going to be alive.

When my second husband died, he gave me coffee and I headed to the bedroom for my quiet time. I came back out into the living room ten minutes later; he was dead on the floor. When he handed me that cup of coffee, neither one of us knew that ten minutes he would be stepping into his eternal life. He was a very faithful servant! He lived his life ready to meet God any minute. I live with the security that one day we will be united.

Father, help us to walk prepared to meet you at any minute. When we get up in the morning, we are never really sure how the day will end. Walk into the day, living our lives like this will be the last minute on this earth. AMEN

LET'S SET THE STAGE:

I have a cousin on my dad's side of the family, her name is Chiquita. Like Connie, we are still so close. We are at my grandparent's. No matter where they lived, they owned an old-time country store.

As children, Chiquita and I would either be outside playing or in her room reading comic books. Her favorite was Archie.

On this particular day we were outside just minding our own business, working our way around the property. You know we were doing important stuff. We got to the feed house; oh, you won't guess what happened next.

We got stopped short in our tracks, on the door to the feed house was the biggest snake I have ever seen even to this day! This snake went all the way up the door across the top and half way down the other side.

We went in and got our grandpa. We dragged him out to the feed house so he could rescue us. We needed rescued and what did he say? Oh girls, that is just a black snake! I want him there he will eat the critters. We didn't care about the critters, AT ALL! In our attempt to be rescued from that snake, he just got to stay right where he was. Not exactly the ending I wanted. Needless to say, we just went around to the other side of the store.

DEVOTION

Then the LORD God said to the woman, 'What is this you have done?' The woman said, 'The serpent deceived me, and I ate.' Genesis 3:13.

I'm sure you could see where this devotion would go. How many of us walk through life not paying attention to the things we are doing or saying?

Things seem to sneak up on us. Our morals are being broken down just a little at a time. In my lifetime we went from a very sheltered life as children, to the state we are in now. For example we stayed out until the sun went down. The change didn't happen overnight. The things we do changed a little at a time. In the 1950's we had very strict rules by which we had to live. In comparison to today's standards, life was a fairy tale. On the outside of the homes were what I called cookie cutter life. Everyone's morals were just about the same. Different religions but about the same in every way. 1960's brought us hippies and love children. Morals were loosened quite a bit. 1970's the chains loosened a little more until we get where we are now. What we used to think as good is evil and what we used to thing as evil somehow became good.

The slide from good to evil was very gradual, so gradual in fact, that most people were in the water that was cool and got used to the heat a little a bit at a time. We never really saw what was coming until one day we woke up and BAM, we are where we are now and our morals are being called into question. The church is the enemy. There used to be no sports on Sunday and Wednesday, stores were all closed on Sunday. I remember in the 1970's when that was lifted. The churches were all up in a roar. Now we head over to them to get our stuff done.

Father, we have come so far downhill we didn't even feel the change. Help us to live our lives pleasing to you. AMEN

LET'S SET THE STAGE:

I'm not sure how old I was in this story! Old enough to really make my sister mad at me.

My sister and I shared a bedroom. There were 4 years between us. *I was da baby girl!* I was really the middle child. Yes, in my head I was neglected. I had a brother that really was the baby and four years between us. I didn't really matter if I was oldest or youngest, my brother and sister learned what not to do from me. You should hear how they talk about me now.

On this day, I had done something so bad (I'm rolling my eyes) that my sister felt she needed to take drastic action! As an adult, I'm sure I deserved being treated so badly.

I was in our bedroom just minding my own business. I'm in the closet getting clothes out. I'm sure that this is what was wrong. I had a habit of pulling out so many changes of clothes and leaving them on the bed for her to put away. That is probably why she was so mad.

She was sneaky for sure and for real. I was really engrossed looking for something to change into. I wasn't looking out for myself. She came in closed the closet door on me and she was loaded to bear with a water pistol. She let me have it. I'm sure she had 5 water pistols and emptied them all on me!! Bless my little heart. I'm sure that it broke my soul, I'm just sure of it.

DEVOTION

When she heard about Jesus, she came up behind him in the crowd and touched his cloak, MARK 5:27

Jesus was in a crowd of people and he felt that someone had touched him and power went out to heal her. It was a woman that had hemorrhaged for twelve years. Jesus was on his was to do a task. The touch from the woman distracted him. The woman was healed instantly.

Have you ever been in the middle of one thing and something else comes up that you need to handle at <u>that exact moment</u>. We get distracted and go off in another way. We should be willing to changed what we are doing if the Holy Spirits is leading us in another direction.

So many times, I have been writing the devotion and get all the way to the prayer and have to go back and go a different direction and delete the whole devotion. I try to live my life listening to the Holy Spirit. He has so many times sent me off in a different direction. I was riding my bike (as an adult) and the Holy Spirit told me to go take something to my neighbor. I had not ever even been to her front door. Well, she had come the week before and yelled at my husband and me over something trivial. I just told the Holy Spirit, "She just yelled at us for nothing." I made a couple more trips around the block arguing and, of course, I stopped by my house and walked next door. It really never pays to argue with the Holy Spirit, because if you walk with the Holy Spirit hand-in-hand you never really win that battle. My neighbor answered the door and apologized for yelling at me and told me she thought she was having a stroke. I stayed with her until the ambulance came.

Father, help us to always walk with the Holy Spirit by our side. Help us to listen to the direction you would have us go. AMEN

That was like a two-fer: two storied rolled into one.

LET'S SET THE STAGE:

This is another story about how badly my sister treated me. She was the oldest and, therefore, the bossiest!

I aways say my sister is weird! I would tell her to her face so I guess it's ok in this book. My siblings and I have a rule, whoever isn't around is the one whos fault it w. is. our mom voiced her opinion about this rule more than once and she didn't like that rule at all. Of course, we made things to seem like they were lots worse than they really were. I'm sure you can tell that isn't the case. LOL!

My sister used to make me sooooo mad! Marilyn hated to sleep on wrinkles in the sheet. **EVERY SINGLE NIGHT**, we would be up around 3 am remaking the bed to get those wrinkles out. I could be in the middle of good dream with me falling off of a perfectly good cliff and I would be jerked back to reality only to get up and have to make that stupid bed. Who in their right mind would wakeup every night to remake the bed. Only my sister! I didn't want to make the bed in the morning for the day.

I could go on and on and on about how my sister treated me so badly. I'm sure I could justify every one of them but, lets face it, these are the memories of a child. I am sure I could come up with some things though.

DEVOTION

Now faith is confidence in what we hope for and assurance about what we do not see. Hebrews 11:1 NIV

Yet again, I wasn't sure how the devotion was to play out and once again in researching scripture, it becomes crystal clear.

Every night my sister woke me up to get the wrinkles out of the bed. I didn't see the wrinkles I didn't even feel the wrinkles. They were not that important to me at all.

How can we describe faith any better than that verse in Hebrews.

In my life people ask just exactly how I know the Bible is true. I believe that the Bible is the true Word of God. I understand there are many translations and many interpretations but, the truth always remains the same. God created man, man disappointed God, time and time again. God even destroyed man. In whole, the world has gone crazy, different from the way the world was when I grew up.

In my mind, the Word of God is just that, the Word of God. How in the world do I know that and how can I have faith in the works of God.? Well, you can't see wind but you can feel it. You can't touch the sun but, you feel the heat. You don't have to see with your own eyes to know that wind blows and the sun is hot. So it is with faith, you don't have to touch the nail holes or the wound in his side to know that Jesus died for our sins. We can feel the power of the Trinity and know how it feels to be free.

Father, without a shadow of a doubt I know that you were truly are Creator and our Savior all in one. Help us to believe the unseen and help us trust what happens in our lives, in the end, will work out for Your good. AMEN

LET'S SET THE STAGE:

On to around Jr High, it didn't get any easier for my parents. I'm just a little older!

My mom had this pet peeve, she hated for us kids to eat ice. I guess for her it was like someone pulling their fingernails down a chalkboard. For those of you that are too young to understand that analogy you really didn't have a good childhood. Just kidding!

On this one day, I kept getting into the freezer and grabbing an ice cube. It was summer and we didn't have air conditioning at that time. That's my story and I'm sticking to it! I almost got caught so many times that day but this one time, I heard my mom coming through the living room. I needed to get out of that freezer fast! I didn't get my head out of the freezer in time and I slammed my nose in the freezer door.

I couldn't tell anything was wrong until a few days later. We were headed to my grandparents on my dad's side and I had sunglasses on. They were really hurting my nose for some reason.

We had a family trait of a honking big nose with a hump in the middle. I no longer have that; but at the time I did. When I got to my grandparents, I looked in the mirror and my nose was bigger than normal and very bruised. I'm not sure how my parents didn't see it. I'm sure I broke my nose. I'm just sure of it!

DEVOTION

The human spirit can endure in sickness, but a crushed spirit who can bear? Proverbs 18:14

Life can be so very hard. Circumstances we aren't responsible for what can hit us in ways we aren't expecting. Life has a way to get in the middle of what we are planning. There is a saying, "People make plans and God laughs". I have found that saying true in all ways.

What plans do you have? Where are you headed. Do you seek God in every area of your life? God takes interest in the very smallest area of your life. I have been in situations that I think this is just too trivial for God to step in. I'm ready to head out the door and I can't find my keys. I'm heading off to church and one of the kids spills Kool-Aid down the front of their shirt. You are ready to pay a bill and the papers are gone. All these things interrupt our plans.

We need to learn to stop take a breath and whisper a prayer. Sometimes I stand in the middle of the room and say "Ok God, what in the world did I do with my keys?". "Ok God, what do you want me to do in this circumstance? Every time I get an answer. I don't always get the answer I want but, everything always it works to his plans.

Father, help us in all circumstances of my life seek your will. You see past the clouds to the rainbow. Give us wisdom to accept the way things go and know in the end things will be ok. AMEN

LET'S SET THE STAGE:

I'm still in Jr High. I had this one friend, Shari. I was always at her house. To this day, we are still best friends. We still cause trouble.

I was staying all night at Shari's house. A lot of times her parents were kind enough to take us shopping. We bought all kinds of stuff. You know, stuff that was important to kids in Jr. High.

One night, we just went from store to store looking planning and plotting. While we were in EVERY store, we decided to spray every cologne on the counter. I'm not even sure how much we had on. All I can say is, it was WAY TOO MUCH!

It was time to pile into her parent's car, it was an hour home. I can still hear her mom asking us what in the world we had come into contact with. Can you imagine an hour ride home with 2 girls who had sprayed so much cologne on themselves? I'm sure they had to roll down all 4 windows just to breathe.

When we got home, we were banned to her bedroom until we both had a very long shower. We couldn't exactly get all the smell off but, you could stand to be in the same room with us. Oh, we sure got into a lot of stuff and still do. Now, we cause more adult trouble but things still seem to happen around us. We just look at each other and laugh.

That's the kind of friend everyone needs. The kind of friend who when you get caught with your hand in the cookie jar, makes up crap to make it seem the most normal thing in the world.

DEVOTION

Oil and perfume make the heart glad, and the sweetness of a friend comes from his earnest counsel. Proverbs 27:9

This verse screamed, "Pick me. Pick Me." Shari and I had very glad and light hearts while we were spraying our way though the shopping plaza. We were not in lots of trouble either.

We have been friends for almost 60 years. Friendships like that are few and far between! A friend is like a diamond that shines the brightest through hard times.

We have many conversations and many laughs. But then we have what we call *car conversations*. As we have car conversations, we are serious and we know that what is said is to be kept within the confines of the proverbial car. We discuss things that are only for our ears.

God gives you friends to seek and find answers in even the darkest times of our lives. Make sure the people you hang around with are the ones that points you in the right direction and don't lead you down the wrong road.

Sometimes the people in our lives are true friends but only lead you to heartache. Trust God's guidance to the friendships he leads for and listen to the still small voice when something doesn't feel right.

FATHER, help us to seek council from you to know our true friends and help us to know the ones that use us in everything they need. AMEN

LET'S SET THE STAGE:

I'm still in Jr High and even I can't believe I did this one. I'm sure my mom kept my dad from killing me that day. Since my kids are grown, I'm not sure of my reaction to this one.

When my dad was pastoring a church 70 miles from our house, we left on Friday night and lived there for the weekend and came home on

Sunday night after church. I'm sure my parents were so tired. They really never had a day off.

On this particular week, my sister had been out during the week and came in later than she was supposed to. Needless to say, she got in trouble. She came back to the bedroom crying and upset. I'm not sure what happened between my parents and her, but, it wasn't good!

Fast forward a few days, I'm not sure what I did but, it wasn't good and I was getting in trouble. NOOOO I just couldn't keep my mouth shut! Before I was about to get my punishment, I looked at my dad and said "another thing, the other night when Marilyn got in trouble, you were wrong". Oh my goodness, I'm not sure why I couldn't keep my stupid mouth shut. I remember that my dad's face got so red!! At that exact moment, my mom had to step in between my dad and me. That didn't happen very often but, I'm sure my mom didn't want my dad to go to prison for murder. She probably saved Little Debby's life that night. I have never forgotten that night. It is like it is etched in my memory never to leave the place it is stored in my brain. MY POOR PARENTS!

DEVOTION

**Just as you who were at one time disobedient to God have now
received mercy as a result of their disobedience,**

Romans 11:30

If I haven't touched on disobedience now would be the time to do it.
I can use this topic all through this book. As we look at our lives, have we
really done all that God has wanted us to do. He has a path laid out for us
from the beginning. He did give us free will to choose the path we want
to go down. I heard an analogy; God has this path all laid out before us.
As we go down that path, we can stay in the direction he wants for us.
When we get off his path, we go down another path and all the things
that he had planned for us don't happen. Things make us stumble, but if
we are smart, we will eventually get back on that path and we continue to
get the blessing we are supposed to get. The thing is, we get our blessing
from that day forward but, what about the blessings we missed out on.
We will really never know what would be in store for us. Those chances
are just gone.

That is what happens to us when we disobey. I certainly got in
trouble and we may never know what I lost but, I'm sure it was vast in
comparison to what happened to me.

*Father, help us to walk in your true will. Help us to always stay on
the path you have laid out for us from the beginning. AMEN*

LET'S SET THE STAGE:

I'm on to High School now, I thought I would never get there. It
was Sunday Morning in Church. Most of my life was centered around
church.

As you can tell, I can never keep my mouth shut! As an adult I still
have problems with that. I'm sure that shocks you but, I have learned to
control it a little now.

This one particular morning my dad was going at it in the pulpit.
I wasn't exactly listening, in fact, I was talking and passing notes in the
back row. The great thing about the back row is, my dad couldn't exactly

see what I was doing. Can you imagine a sophomore sitting in front, on that stage. That sends chills down my back now just thinking about it!!! Anyway, I kept a good record of tv shows and the commercials. My dad was trying to make an illustration of a current commercial. He was just preaching along and I was just talking and passing notes. He stopped and asked me what that commercial was he was trying to think of. Lucky for me, one of my friends just happened to listen to that part of the sermon and whispered the answer to me. Whew, that was a very close one. What can I say, we all should be grateful for those who come to our rescue!!!

DEVOTION

But a Samaritan, as he traveled, came where the man was; and when he saw him, he took pity on him. Luke 10:33

Some of us know the story of the Samaritan. A man was lying on the side of the road robbed and beaten and left for dead. Two religious leaders passed by and did nothing. They just kept on walking. It was a Samaritan that was on a journey that stopped and helped the man. He made sure he was cared for.

Samaritans were not liked very well. They came from a very poor tribe. Their religion was a mix of pagan worship and God worship. The religious leaders did not care to stop and help this man. In my mind they just couldn't be bothered, they left him for dead.

The Samaritan was humble and carried him to the next town and made sure there was someone to take care of him.

How are we living our lives. Do we pass by when we see others in need? I have a group of friends that walk the talk of Jesus Christ. We see a need and if we can help, we all step in and try with everything we have to meet that need.

Father, help us to always be an example of the life you gave us. If there is a need, help us to step in and make sure that need is met. AMEN

LET'S SET THE STAGE:

There is not an age to this story. This could be any time that we kids got in trouble when we were a little older.

From these stories you would think I would just not want to get in trouble. With me, I just never learned my lesson.

I'm going to give you a run down on every time one of us was in trouble. In my head, when most of you got in trouble it was just the one time get a spanking and you were done. NOT AT OUR HOUSE. It was an all-night thing. Never stopped me but, it did take all night.

There was the wait till your dad get home and then when he walks into the house, mom filled him in on the day and so it began.

The first thing was the talk. We had to hear a recap of what we did. It's not like we didn't know it but we had to relive it for a very long time! Then came the spanking. It was never too traumatic, but a spanking none the less.

Next came the "now go to your room" where we stayed until what I'm guessing my mom said "Now Jr, that's long enough" and he let us come out of our room.

On to the next stage, we had to tell our mom we were sorry and then we did get to join the family but, we couldn't talk (that one was hard for me). We had to think about what we had done. You can bet one thing for sure; I had been thinking about what I had done ever since my mom said "wait till your dad gets home". I pretended to think about it and then there was the prayer. We always had to ask God to forgive us. Me, I just ask God to forgive me, then in my head, I would ask forgiveness for everything I didn't get caught doing. I just wanted to cover my bases.

DEVOTION

Whoever spares the rod hates their children, but the one who loves their children is careful to discipline them. Proverbs 13:24

I know this is a controversial subject. Spankings are taboo but let's break this down.

To spare the rod means not to always spank. I have heard some people say, "My kids are my best friend!" Really? My best friend and I went to Jr High together. We have been through so much stuff and stayed the test of time. My kids on the other hand, as adults we are more like friends but, I am still the parent.

If we don't discipline our kids in some fashion, it makes them think that they are above the law and we end up with kids that are out of control. Our society is in crisis Spanking is not always the answer. I used a lot of different things to discipline my kids. I really do miss the period in my life when I had the cleanest baseboard in America, maybe even the world. The whole lesson in this is that it's not wrong to discipline our kids, it's wrong to beat our kids. We all need to find a way to let our kids know when they are misbehaving.

Father, we are at a crossroad in the world where good is evil and evil is good. Help us to set the example for our kids and give us the tools to show them the right way and the only way is through you. AMEN

LET'S SET THE STAGE:

I was in about third or fourth grade in this story. I lived less than a mile from school so I was a walker. Let me just get this out of my system, the next block down was a mile. I only lived three houses from the end of the block. I never really agreed with that one-mile rule. I didn't make the rules, I just always seemed to break them.

The school district was good enough to fix us a pea gravel path along the road. It was a really good path. Usually, I walked on the path singing hymns at the top of my lungs. I can carry a tune.

As always, there is an exception to everything I do on normal days. This one day they were blacktopping the road. I'm sure you know what is coming next. Yep, I did it. That black gooey tar was just too hard to resist. I walked all the way to the entrance of the subdivision in the tar. There was the occasional car so at that point I got on the path. So, not only did I have thick tar on my shoes, but gravel in the mix.

We had light tan carpet and I didn't think anything about walking into the house. I'm sure my mom had a second sense about what was coming where I was concerned. Somehow, she was outside when I got home. She took one look at my shoes and I don't think I had to wait till my dad got home for this offence. She had a great come apart right there in the front yard, followed by a come to Jesus' moment for me. I don't remember what form of punishment was dished out. Whatever it was, it was just. I'm also sure that it wasn't enough for my crime.

DEVOTION

Come,' he said. Then Peter got down out of the boat, walked on the water and came toward Jesus. Matthew 14:29

I didn't walk on water or anything and to be quite fair, it was downright sticky and yucky. I did have faith that I would just keep walking. It never occurred to me that I might just walk out of my shoes.

In Matthew, Jesus was walking on the water and Peter wanted to do likewise. He asked Jesus if he could walk on the water. He didn't just get out of the boat; he asked the Creator if he could help him to do as Jesus did. He had such a glad heart to follow in Jesus' steps and actually defy the norm and walk on water. He took his eyes off of Jesus and he began to sink.

How many times in our lives have we asked God to give us something and he grants our wishes. We have the very best of intentions and we suddenly get bored or scared and take our eyes off of God and we begin to sink in the water. He gives us our hearts desire and we look away for a moment and we fall.

Father, as we ask for things help us to know where and what you want out of our lives. As we walk in the path you have allowed us to go down, help us not to ever take our eyes off you. Give us a desire to always walk toward you and the plans you have laid out for us. AMEN

LET'S SET THE STAGE:

We have established that I was quite the stinker, I still am and proud of it! This story is Christmas in first or second grade.

I was so hard on shoes. You know one must drag your toes as you walk down the sidewalk. It's just a must for a little girl like me. My parents got so tired of buying me shoes. I think it was Red Wing Shoes that had that were almost indestructible. That is what I started getting.

One Christmas I got these little booties. I remember them so vividly! They were black. I remember trying my best to take care of them. No way was I dragging my toes in those booties.

I got to wear them to my grandparent's house down the street. I was so proud. I went around to Grandma and Grandpa and all my aunt's and uncle's to show them. I got to my Uncle Leon, I just had to prove they were new, I just had to! I had heard my dad talk about a thing called new car smell. I got really quiet and my parents were busy visiting with everyone. They should have known by now that if I get quiet trouble is just around the corner. My cousin Connie must not have been there or I would have been busy with her. I looked around the room to see whom my victim might be. There he was sitting on that green couch. I mean he was visiting a little but I took my opportunity at a lull in the conversation.

Poor Uncle Leon, He was always a good sport but I don't think he appreciated it much when I took my shoe off and shoved it under his nose. About that time my dad rounded the corner and I heard "Deborah Ann." I didn't get a whoppin' but, I did get taken into the kitchen and got a stern talking to. My dad had this look on his face when he meant business. To be sure his face was red as it could be. I remember him asking what in the world I was doing, I said I had to prove my shoes were new. He just shook his head in disbelief. I told him that I heard him talking about new car smell and I was sure that my shoes had that new shoe smell. What could he say, not much after that. You would think he would have learned by now that you had to watch what you said in front of me. See, it wasn't my fault after all.

DEVOTION

On coming to the house, they saw the child with his mother Mary, and they bowed down and worshiped him. Then they opened their treasures and presented him with gifts of gold, frankincense and myrrh. Matthew 2:11

This was a Christmas story so it seems to fit that I would use this verse for the story. In our story at Christmas this happened when he was in the manager. In reality it was around two years later. This can be proven in this verse at the beginning it says "On coming to the house."

I'm going to use a little imagination here and try to see this from Mary's point- of- view. She was visited by an angel to tell her she had be chosen to carry the Son of God. That alone would have sent me packing. With honor, she accepted this. She had to ride a donkey across country while carrying a baby in her last months. She got to Bethlehem and knew she was carrying the Christ child. She had to give birth in a stable and put this sweet innocent baby in a manger of hay.

Two years later, wisemen show up and present gold, frankincense and myrrh. Frankincense, is a resin that when looked upon had a glittery look, it was used in religious ceremony it had a distinct smell. Myrrh had a strong smell and was used in the embalming process. I have heard that these gifts may have been prophesying his life. The Gold for royalty, Frankincense his divinity and the Myrrh representing Jesus' death on the cross.

Father, you sent you son to earth to live a human life. For three years he showed his purpose on Earth only to be made a living sacrifice for our sins. Thank you, Father, you sent you Son to Earth to live a human life.

For three years loving us enough to send your son to bear all our sins. Thank you, Father for having us enough to your Son to bear all the sins on His Shoulders, suffered and died with us on his mind. AMEN

LET'S SET THE STAGE:

I was in sixth grade; I only remember this because you had to be in sixth grade for this privilege. A couple of weeks before I was to start at school, my mom got a phone call from the school. They had chosen me to be a patrol person. I bet they heard how I handled things that day they were putting tar on the road. I did it with pride, I really did.

I had to go to school a week early and "get trained" they handed us the straps that we were to wear when we were at our stations. It was white and went around my waist, (I was so skinny that it just kinda hung down) went up my back and went down at a diagonal across my chest. This was an honor and I carried myself as if it were the greatest responsibility I had ever had. It probably was at that time in my life.

First day at school, I was on the corner of the road with the tar and the road to school. It was my responsibility to stop traffic and let the kids cross the road. I was large and in charge, right there! I actually got to stop cars! I just couldn't get over the fact that when I put my hand up the adults just stopped. They listened to a little, and I do mean little girl and actually put their foot on that pedal that made the car stop. I had seen it before but it had never been a thing for me. I had power that the 1-5 grade kids didn't. I never saw one of those kids stop traffic. In my head I was to cool for school. I probably weighed 60 pounds and I had the power!!!!! It was a great responsibility that was entrusted to me. I took it very seriously and my mom was very proud of me.

DEVOTION

When his parents saw him, they were astonished. His mother said to him, "Son, why have you treated us like this? Your father and I have been anxiously searching for you." "Why were you searching for me?" he asked. "Didn't you know I had to be in my Father's house?"
Luke 2:48-49

Even as a child Jesus understood the responsibility he had on his life. In this passage, Jesus got separated from Mary and Joseph. Can you imagine how frantic they must have been. I remember getting separated from my kids in a crowd and I was so happy when my eyes saw my children.

Jesus had a responsibility on Him like no one else had before or after in history. The priests were amazed at the knowledge Jesus possessed. How could a child know the things he did. HE HAD THE POWER! You know me so well; I sang that in my head and I bet you did too!

Jesus grew up to teach only the priest didn't like it that he taught in such different way. Life is that way, we can't please everyone nor do we want. We must do as Jesus did and live our lives in a manner that would please God.

Father, please walk with us as we wander down this path of life. Help us to be ever close to you and show us how you want us to live our lives to show glory and love. Captivate us with everything you have and give us the knowledge to walk on the path that you have prepared for us. AMEN

LET'S SET THE STAGE:

In one of my other stories, we established that my brother could tell "jokes". In this story he got it after his little "joke".

My mom and dad had to go somewhere and my sister and I weren't home and David didn't want to go. With much hesitation they left him home by himself. When my parents got home, he had a joke to end all jokes.

According to my brother, while my parents were gone, my dad's brother stopped by. Boy, did they ever have a great time. They horsed around, popped popcorn and watched a movie. My dad was little upset that he missed his brother but, oh well, he will see him another time.

My dad was a downtown St. Louis, MO truck driver and my uncle worked building downtown buildings. By chance, one day my dad and Uncle Don saw each other. My dad said, Donnie, I'm sorry I missed you a couple of weeks ago. Uncle Don had a funny look on his face and asked my dad what he was talking about. My dad said "the night Christina and I were gone and you and David popped popcorn and watched a movie. To that, Uncle Don said "Jr, I never came out to your house."

Whoopie, David had finally done it. He couldn't say "can't you take a joke" and get out of it. David didn't have the privilege of hearing my mom say, "wait till your dad gets home. He didn't know that when my dad got home, he was in for the night of his life. You know the whole ordeal of us getting a spanking. I got the pleasure of sitting back and 1) watch someone else be the one in trouble and 2) watch my brother get his just desserts finally for all those other times. I know what you are going to tell me, it's not nice for me to be happy about someone else getting in trouble. He deserved it after all those other times he didn't get in trouble. Or was it that I was just mad because I never thought to add "can't you take a joke". Well, anyway he got it and wrong or not, I was happy on the inside.

DEVOTION

I applied my heart to what I observed and learned a lesson from what I saw: Proverbs 24:32

I knew I couldn't do another devotion on lying or not minding so when this verse popped up, I grabbed it.

I didn't need to observe my brother lie and get away with it. He did that plenty and boy oh boy, did I ever get mad. You see, I watched him get away with it time and time again! You can be sure I saw that and didn't lie that was where I draw the line. I might me stubborn, strong-willed, and on and on; but, I did not lie.

I might be all those things but I sat back and observed a lot, for sure! I watched and waited; I think I to see what I could get away with. For that, I am sure! I don't think that waiting for my brother to get caught was to far out of my wheel house. I just stood around the corner and giggled. Finally, he got caught. Although, now it seems petty but in the then it was great.

My brother and I are very close. We share all kinds of things brother's and sister's share. I thank God every day for him. To this day I stand back and watch. To be sure, I now don't want people to get themselves in a jam but, it is just human nature. Let's just say with much experience comes much insight into how to live my life. I'm sure that is how it is with everyone. I conducted myself different when my first husband died than I did when my second husband.

We grow and we learn as we watch. Be ever mindful that the Lord is watching and seeing how we conduct ourselves. Right or wrong, he is a forgiving God.

Father, help us to watch and learn and always be mindful of our words and actions. Help us to set an example that is worthy of you. AMEN

Don't miss out!

Visit the website below and you can sign up to receive emails whenever Debby Hadley Triplett publishes a new book. There's no charge and no obligation.

https://books2read.com/r/B-A-JMSVC-DBSIF

Connecting independent readers to independent writers.

About the Author

Debby is a lighthearted fun person to be around. She loves to joke and tease. One thing about Debby is that you will never be bored when you are around her.

One year for Christmas, her son bought her a ring that she had sent him a link to, and it ended up being really big. He said "You didn't need to send the link. We Googled rings for crazy, old, purple haired women". To that she just said "Hey, who you are calling old. She knew the other two things she couldn't deny. On another occasion they had a Family Fall Festival at her church. She bought a long red wig and wore all Kahki clothes with black shoes. What do you think she was trying to be? "normal" All she could say was it was the worse one minute of her life.

Debby has lost 2 husbands. Her last husband, Steve died in 2020 of complications to COVID. It was an extremely hard road back. Her faith is all that has sustained her. God brought he through and she has her happy back. Besides writing, Debby illustrates children's book. She is actually busier now than when she worked a full-time job.

Well, there you have it, Debby all tied up with a bow on her head.